MANCHESTER AIRPORT
RINGWAY REMEMBERED

Arranged alongside the International Pier in the mid-1960s are Viscounts G-AOHH of BEA, G-AOCC of British Eagle and what appears to be an 800 series Viscount of Aer Lingus. On the Domestic Pier is another BEA Viscount, the registration on this aircraft is still on the tip of the tail whereas on G-AOHH it is below the insignia in much larger letters. The new administration block behind the control tower has not yet been built. Many spectators can be seen on the public viewing terraces. At this time a charge was levied on spectators to use each pier.

MANCHESTER AIRPORT
RINGWAY REMEMBERED

Barry Abraham and Les Jones

TEMPUS

Tempus Publishing Limited
The Mill, Brimscombe Port,
Stroud, Gloucestershire, GL5 2QG

ISBN 0 7524 2109 3

Typesetting and origination by
Tempus Publishing Limited
Printed in Great Britain by
Midway Clark Printing, Wiltshire

Capitol Airways Inc. was amongst a number of American airlines such as Transocean, TWA, Seaboard & Western and Flying Tiger which were chartered to return families home from the American base at Burtonwood, near Warrington, while it was running down prior to complete closure as a USAF base. These airlines operated Constellations and Super Constellations into Ringway and Capitol L-1049G N4903C is representative. A couple of other American Airlines, also not seen previously at Ringway, were Slick Airways and Overseas National Airways which used DC-6As on these flights.

Contents

Acknowledgements

Most of the photographs for this book have been taken by the authors or loaned. Unfortunately, a number which have been donated to their collections over the years did not identify the photographer. We have tried to establish this but in some cases it has eluded us. We are sorry if any credit has not been given. In our search for relevant photographs to fill in some of the gaps, we are especially indebted to Harry Holmes, Brian R.Robinson, Terry Holden, Sue Redmond of British Airways Public Relations, Manchester, and David Antrobus of Northern Executive Aviation. We also wish to thank A.N. Angus, Leo Carter, Alan Charlesworth, Tom Clarke, G.P. Gass, Don Moores, H. Parrish, Stanley Thirwall for their photographs, Geoff Simmons, for his help in printing some of the older photographs from poor negatives, and Ray Towler, who drew the plan of Ringway.

Certain photographs, advice and help from Patsy McClements and Paul Isherwood of the Manchester Airport Archive were most useful.

A number of books have been consulted to check information. They are: *British Independent Airlines Since 1946* Vols I to IV, by Tony Merton Jones; *Illustrated History of BEA*, by Phil Lo Bo; *Early Ringway*, by Ray Webb; *First and Foremost*, by Steve McDonald, *Aviation in Manchester,* by Brian R.Robinson. In addition, various books published by Air-Britain detailing airliner history and other documents have been used to help captioning events, and airline and aircraft histories.

This book is dedicated to Brian R. Robinson, leading Manchester aviation historian, who cooperated in the compilation of this book.

Few photographs are available of aircraft at Wythenshawe. This Avro 504K G-EBKB of Berkshire Aviation Tours Ltd (a company operated by F.J.V. Holmes) based at Monkmoor Aerodrome, Shrewsbury is believed to be at Wythenshawe. The company amalgamated with Northern Airlines Ltd in 1929 and transferred its sphere of operations to Barton.

Introduction

Since the early days of flying there has been a tremendous fascination with aircraft and most public demonstrations drew attention from a large crowd. In the United Kingdom, regular passenger services were slow to develop but, in the years after the Second World War, Manchester Airport became an important centre of airline services and is now a world-status airport. The day-to-day operations have provided a popular spectator activity. This interest caused the authors to put together their memories through photographs of the aircraft and people who worked at Ringway.

Both authors have been engaged with recording the history of Ringway and have seen the tremendous developments which have taken place over the past fifty years or so. Barry Abraham's interest in aviation began in 1952, when, during his schooldays, helped to form the Ringway Spotters Club with a number of other enthusiasts. His business life was spent with an insurance broking and risk management company in Manchester, until early retirement a few years ago. Les Jones joined the airline business at Speke airport, Liverpool, during the Second World War, working for the Associated Airways Joint Committee, which controlled the limited air routes within Great Britain at the time. He then moved to Ringway, becoming a member of the management structure of British European Airways. He also formed the first flying club to be based at Ringway.

This fitting memorial to commemorate the first non-stop transatlantic flight was unveiled at Ringway on 29 October 1964 by the Lord Mayor of Manchester. John Alcock and Arthur Whitten Brown flew the Atlantic on 14 June 1919. They were both Manchester men (although Brown had been born in Glasgow) and were subsequently knighted.

Taken in 1944, this view shows the camouflaged terminal building and hangars with an array of ATA taxi Ansons and a Dakota of the Parachute Training School.

Air France Dakota F-BAXG seen on 3 April 1953. The company, one of the first overseas airlines to use Ringway, had used the type at Ringway since 1946. In 1954, Air France replaced the Dakotas with Viscounts on the Paris service.

One

Early Days: 1919-1945

A small aerodrome existed in Trafford Park, now covered by industrial development, and during the First World War, the Royal Flying Corps/Royal Air Force opened a large aerodrome near Withington, known as the Alexandra Park, as an Aircraft Acceptance Park for aircraft built at the National Aircraft Factory No.2, Heaton Chapel, Stockport. It was also used by A.V. Roe & Co. Ltd, a company which had been building aircraft in Manchester since 1910.

On 1 May 1919 the first air service to Manchester (Alexandra Park Aerodrome) commenced from Cricklewood, London by Handley Page Transport Ltd using a converted O/400 bomber. A few weeks later, on 26 May, the first UK scheduled domestic service was initiated by the Avro Transport Company using an Avro 504 to Southport Sands, then on to Blackpool South Shore. On 22 October 1922 the first sustained internal UK air route to London (Croydon) was opened and it was flown by Daimler Airways using a de Havilland DH.34.

Alexandra Park aerodrome survived until 1924 when use of the land was required for other purposes, its existence is commemorated by a plaque on a building located on the site which is now used mainly as a sports field. The loss of the aerodrome and its hangars was a blow to the development of air services to Manchester but the City Council selected land at Barton Moss, near Eccles, for development as a civic airport. A temporary aerodrome at Wythenshawe (now covered by housing) was opened while the new airport was built. The first landing at Wythenshawe was made on 2 April 1929, it was the first municipal aerodrome in the United Kingdom to receive an Air Ministry licence, granted on 19 April to be effective from 22 April 1929.

The new airport was to be known as Manchester Municipal Airport. It operated from 1 January 1930, with a formal opening on 1 June 1930. Northern Air Lines (Manchester) Ltd was appointed to manage it and brought in a large fleet of aircraft, mainly Avro 504s. At the beginning a large steel and brick hangar was built. The control tower, with a Radio Direction Finding station and meteorological office, followed in 1933.

Imperial Airways Ltd commenced a subsidized service in June 1930 on the route Croydon – Birmingham (Castle Bromwich) – Manchester (Barton) – Liverpool (Speke) using Armstrong Whitworth Argosy and Handley Page airliners, but the service did not continue after the end of 1930. Railway Air Services Ltd opened a trunk air route linking London, the Midlands, Northern Ireland and Scotland, using the de Havilland DH.86 Express and DH.89 Dragon Rapide aircraft ordered for use on the services. Manchester (Barton) Airport was included in the schedules beginning on 20 August 1934.

KLM-Royal Dutch Airlines was approached by Manchester Corporation in 1934 to include Manchester in its service between Amsterdam and Liverpool but they felt Barton was too small. This comment led to the eventual development of a larger airport at Ringway. Fairey Aviation Ltd, which had taken over the old National Aircraft Factory at Heaton Chapel in Stockport, built their own hangar just before the new airport was ready. Manchester (Ringway) Airport was formally opened on Saturday 25 June 1938 by Sir Kingsley Wood, the Secretary of State for Air. Services and passenger facilities were transferred, and an announcement was made that Ringway would be a junction airport in a new system of internal air services. Scheduled operations began on Monday 27 June by Railway Air Services which left for Liverpool (Speke)

Airport to connect with the Isle of Man service. KLM introduced their service, calling at Ringway *en route* from Amsterdam to Dublin and return.

At the beginning of 1939, No.613 Squadron (City of Manchester) Auxiliary Air Force was formed using a farm building as an office and taking over part of a newly-erected Bellman hangar by the terminal building. A.V. Roe & Co. Ltd at Woodford needed additional space and took over hangars to house their development and experimental department. Ringway was not requisitioned during the Second World War but, with the agreement of the Corporation, was used extensively by the military. Many buildings were erected with the intention of being converted for civil purposes after the war. Ringway became home of the Parachute Training School and a number of small units involved with airborne landings which trained paratroopers using a dropping zone at nearby Tatton Park.

National Air Communications (later Associated Airways Joint Committee) used Barton for a service to Dublin, using de Havilland DH.86B flown by West Coast Air Services Ltd in association with Aer Lingus Teoranta, until 15 November 1942 when the UK terminal was transferred to Liverpool (Speke) Airport.

The North West made a major contribution to aircraft production during the war and, in order to ferry aircraft from the manufacturers, the Air Transport Auxiliary stationed a pool (No.14) at Ringway, all types of aircraft were to be seen on their dispersals *en route* to various parts of the country.

Fairey Aviation extended their premises to cater for the increased flow of aircraft built at Heaton Chapel. These hangars survived until recent years but now only two remain. Three large hangars were also built on the south side of the Airport for A.V.Roe & Co. Ltd, initially for the production of the Avro York airliner. These buildings were later used for a variety of purposes but were eventually demolished to make way for the Second Runway Project.

The Handley Page O/400 D8350 (a temporary civil use of its former military serial number), of Handley Page Transport Ltd, is probably at Cricklewood, London. It was used on the first air service to Alexandra Park Aerodrome, on 1 May 1919, the day it received its Certificate of Airworthiness and also the day that Air Navigation Regulations came into force to control civil flying. Later in the year this aircraft was used by the company to inaugurate their London to Paris air service.

Little remains to show the existence of Alexandra Park Aerodrome alongside Princess Road, Withington. Now known as Houghend Fields, the area is used for various sporting facilities. This plaque was placed on the sports club building to commemorate the first aerodrome within Manchester.

The new airport at Barton was to be known as Manchester Municipal Airport. It operated from 1 January 1930, with a formal opening on 1 June 1930. The large Municipal Hangar built in 1929, which still remains, was in use right from the beginning.

The Municipal Hangar does not enjoy any heritage 'listing' status. However, to mark the seventieth anniversary of the opening of the Airport, this plaque, fixed to the building, was unveiled on 29 January 2000.

The Handley Page HP.42 Heracles G-AAXC of Imperial Airways visited Barton in the mid-1930s but the company did not operate any services from Barton at this time. This particular aircraft is noteworthy in that it was the first commercial aircraft in the world to have flown one million miles in passenger service – in 1937.

Popular airliners of the day were the de Havilland Dragon (left) and Dragon Rapide (right), at Barton in June 1937. The temporary Fairey Aviation hangars constructed next to the Municipal Hangar were used for the final assembly of Fairey Battles before this work was transferred to Ringway.

The de Havilland Dragon G-ACHV was used by Railway Air Services Ltd between 1935 and 1936 at Barton, on the Manx route. It replaced an aircraft which had been written off in a crash after taking off from Ronaldsway Airport, Isle of Man, en route to Liverpool, and then Manchester. The control tower and meteorological office built in 1933 with a Radio Direction Finding station still remains in use but has now lost the radio aerials, these being dismantled in the 1960s.

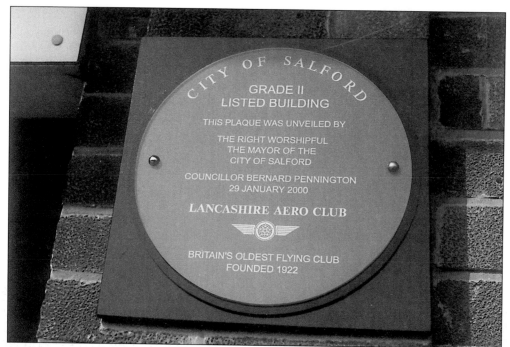

The airport is within the bounds of the City of Salford, although the land was originally leased by the Manchester Corporation. Enjoying the status of a Grade II listed building, this special plaque was also unveiled on 29 January 2000.

The de Havilland DH.86B Express G-AEWR of Railway Air Services, named *Venus*, was present on the opening day at Ringway, landing on 25 June 1938, and was a regular visitor on various flights. It is seen here at Liverpool (Speke) Airport during 1938 being used on services between Croydon, Ringway, Speke, Isle of Man, Belfast and Glasgow.

The new terminal building, control tower and hangar at Ringway with a de Havilland DH.89 Dragon Rapide of Isle of Man Air Services on the small apron. At this time the entire airfield was grass covered, runways not being completed until 1942. Spectators are on the roof terraces, the airport still caters for the viewing public.

Awaiting the first flight of the prototype Avro 679 Manchester bomber, in July 1939, are three of the key people involved in the development of the aircraft. From left to right they are: Charlie Hatton (Production Manager), Sandy Jack (Chief Inspector), Stuart Davies (Assistant Chief Designer). During the war the prototype Avro Lancaster, York and Lincoln had their first flight at Ringway.

Barracuda LS855 was signalled as being ready for collection on 24 June 1944. On the apron in front of the control tower it awaits ferrying by No.14 Ferry Pool ATA. Between August 1944 and February 1945, it was with No.812 Squadron, coded 'N1H'. By May 1945 it was with No.783 Squadron at Arbroath. Its fate is unknown, but it was presumably scrapped soon after the war ended. Anson taxi aircraft and a visiting Airspeed Oxford await their crews.

Ferrying of aircraft from manufacturers to RAF units, when operational, or to maintenance units, was mainly carried out by the Air Transport Auxiliary, a largely forgotten, civilian-manned service. Ringway was the base of No.14 Ferry Pool (FP). They used a number of aircraft to position pilots, especially the Avro Anson. Their offices were in the terminal building and they used Bellman Hangar No.3.

A locally-built aircraft was the Bristol Beaufighter by Fairey Aviation. The ATA not only collected aircraft built at Ringway but also used the airport as a staging post. This photograph of a Beaufighter with an ATA crew standing in front appears to have been taken on the dispersal area to the north-west of the terminal buildings and hangars, a site now occupied by Terminal Two aprons.

The Control Tower building in 1944, also the Headquarters of No.14 FP. A board marks the designation of the runway in use and the brick defensive post in front of the building is evident.

A.V. Roe & Co. Ltd began planning a civil airliner in 1943 and the Tudor, designed for the North Atlantic route, was subsequently ordered by the Government for the nationalized airlines. The prototype had its first flight at Ringway on 14 June 1945 piloted by Bill Thorn and Jimmy Orrell, it was unmarked but had the military serial TT176 allotted and became civil registered as G-AGPF. Avro closed their Ringway Experimental Department in November 1946 and transferred it to Woodford.

Two
Civil Flying
Recommences:
1946-1948

At the end of the war, Manchester Corporation regained full control of the airport and civil flying recommenced in 1946 with a number of charter flights. Scheduled airline operations began in June by an Air France Douglas DC-3 Dakota. On 29 July 1946 Railway Air Services used an Avro 19 Anson on the service Croydon – Ringway – Belfast which was taken over by British European Airways.

A.V. Roe & Co. Ltd closed their Ringway operation and transferred it to Woodford, their main base. Avro had used Ringway for the first prototype flights of the Avro Manchester, Lancaster and Lincoln bombers, York transport and Tudor airliner aircraft. During the war, Fairey Aviation had produced large numbers of Battle, Fulmar and Barracuda aircraft to their own design, and Beaufighter and Halifax aircraft under contract, but continued to use Ringway afterwards for production and aircraft engineering.

Sivewright Airways Ltd, a local company, did various charter flights with services to the Isle of Man, and Jersey, in the Channel Islands, being most popular. Douglas Dakotas were obtained and the company also participated in the Berlin Airlift. In 1947, KLM reintroduced their service to Amsterdam, and on to Dublin, with Aer Lingus operating a similar service, both airlines using the Douglas DC-3 Dakota. Other continental services were started in 1948.

No.613 Squadron had reformed on 10 May 1946 and operated Supermarine Spitfires. Alongside them from October 1949 were the Austers of No.1951 Flight in the Air Observation Post role.

Railway Air Services Ltd, which had operated into Ringway before the war, recommenced services on 29 July 1946 to and from Croydon Airport and Belfast. This Avro 19 G-AHIC, seen here on 23 January 1947, was used. Routes of Railway Air Services Ltd and other airlines became part of British European Airways Corporation on 1 February 1947. Noteworthy is the evidence of camouflage on the Control Tower building and the concrete apron 'toned down' from the wartime period.

Scheduled services between Manchester and Paris were inaugurated by Air France in June 1946. In later months the service was operated on their behalf by Scottish Airlines. Air France began to use their own aircraft again in 1947 and seen here is Dakota F-BAXI being refuelled on 5 March 1947. The Air France flag was flown from above the cockpit when the aircraft was on the ground.

Caudron Goeland of the French Air Force, serialled 1273, visited on 15 March 1947. It is on the small apron in front of the terminal building. This is not the usual version of the Goeland, in that the height of the fuselage has been increased and an additional set of windows installed.

A number of ship's crews charters used Ringway with Det Norske Luftfartselskap AS and Fred Olsen Air Transport, both based in Oslo, operated Douglas Dakotas. This could have been Norwegian Airlines (DNL) LN-IAM which visited on 13 June 1947, the following day Fred Olsen used LN-NAD. The checkerboard flag being flown from the Control Tower is believed to signify Air Traffic Control, where pilots are to report on arrival.

In July 1947 Aer Lingus started a service to and from Dublin and Amsterdam, via Ringway, using Dakotas in a variety of schemes until they settled on a common colour scheme. Named *St Bridgid*, Douglas Dakota EI-ACH carries one of the early schemes on 1 July 1947.

Marshall's Flying School Ltd, of Cambridge, had begun charter work to supplement their engineering and flying school activities. Like many other similar firms they provided an 'air taxi' between UK airports carrying business people, members of the Press and race-goers. On 24 July 1947, Dragon Rapide G-AHED called while on a flight from Cambridge to Belfast.

The Royal Netherlands Naval Air Service (MLD) operated the Fairey Firefly and ordered some more aircraft. The work being shared with Fairey's other factories. During 1947 a B-25 Mitchell, serialled 2-1, of the RNNAS brought ferry pilots from Valkenberg, in Holland, to collect modified Fireflies. The aircraft is taxiing past Hangar No.7, usually all quiet outside during weekdays!

Fairey Aviation also overhauled and prepared a large number of de Havilland Mosquitoes for service with the Turkish Air Force between 1947 and 1948. This aircraft is on the terminal apron but, other than nationality markings, its individual identity is not clear.

Beside the main entrance of the 1938 terminal building entrance hall was the reception desk manned by BEA staff, with the customary scales and Conditions of Carriage.

BEA maintained an operations room to log the position of each flight, in addition, it was necessary to work on aircraft load sheets. The office was located on the first floor of the 1938 terminal building and here Ship's Papers Clerk John Evans is seen hard at work on 13 November 1947.

BEA used the de Havilland Dragon Rapide on services to and from the Isle of Man, which also included Blackpool in the schedule. Being refuelled is G-AGSJ which had originally been civilianized for Associated Joint Airways Committee, then taken over by Isle of Man Air Services in 1945, before coming into BEA during February 1947.

Avro 19 G-AHXK, named *Mancunia*, operated by Sivewright Airways Ltd and flown by Captain Ainsworth, in from Jersey, on 10 July 1948. The company operated three Avro 19s with a number of other aircraft and was based at Ringway and Barton.

One of the great Ringway characters was Bruce Martin who flew Dragon Rapides for Sivewright Airways. He is seen here with G-AJMY. When the company closed, Bruce Martin bought one of the Dragon Rapides G-AGDM and used it on charter work and pleasure flying for Airviews Ltd.

Sivewright Airways Ltd also used a Taylorcraft Plus D G-AHHY for photographic work. It was a wartime Taylorcraft Auster converted for civilian use. The lady is the mother of co-author Les Jones. The picture was taken on the apron in front of the 1938 terminal building, with the Bellman hangar, erected just before the war, in the background.

BEA Dakota G-AHCV with the double door open, unloading freight onto the trolleys. This aircraft was recorded on 21 January 1948 operating the Speke Airport, Liverpool, to Ringway then on to Northolt, London, service. Northolt effectively replaced Croydon as the London Airport for internal UK and European flights in 1947.

Sabena Dakota OO-UBT made its first visit to Ringway on 10 June 1948. The aircraft had been registered OO-CBT but certain records indicate that the aircraft was not registered as OO-UBT until December that year! However, unless there was a switch in airframes at one point, a Dakota registered as OO-UBT crashed after take-off on 21 April 1988 at Quelimane, Mozambique, possibly shot down!

Airspeed Envoys had been used before the war by a number of airlines and the type formed the basis of the military Oxford trainer (many of which were civilianized after the war as the Airspeed Consul). The RAF did order a number of Envoys for communications duties, including P5626, which came onto the British civil register as G-AHAC after the war, operated by Private Charter Ltd, of Heston Airport, near London. It visited Ringway on 1 March 1948.

Beech Expeditor OO-APO of John Mahieu Aviation, on a wet 8 April 1948, prior to departure to Melsbroek, the airport of Brussels.

Alitalia extended their Rome to London (Northolt) service on to Ringway in April 1948 using Savoia Marchetti SM.95 aircraft. Unfortunately, the service was not a success and was suspended the following month. Seen on 8 April 1948 is I-DALL which had arrived the previous day and stayed overnight.

Newcastle-upon-Tyne Aero Club was re-formed after the war and operated from Woolsington, the Newcastle Airport, with a fleet of three Tiger Moths and two Austers. This Tiger Moth, seen at Ringway in 1948, became well known at various air races for many years. In fact, on 12 July 1958, when flown by Jim Denyer, it won the Kings Cup Air Race at Baginton Airport, Coventry. A Sivewright Dakota is in the back of the hangar.

Air Show day on 24 April 1948, organized by No.613 Squadron, brought Lord Tedder in this Dakota KJ994. It was attached to No.24 Squadron based at Bassingbourn, in Cambridgeshire, and named *Dulcie*. The five star insignia of Lord Tedder can be seen above the tail nationality markings.

The air show on 24 April 1948 also produced a number of visitors. British Nederland Air Services Ltd, based at Tollerton Airport, Nottingham, had just taken delivery of two Douglas Dakotas for services and charter work from Bovingdon Airport, in the London area. It called at Ringway from Tollerton, then went on to Hendon aerodrome, London.

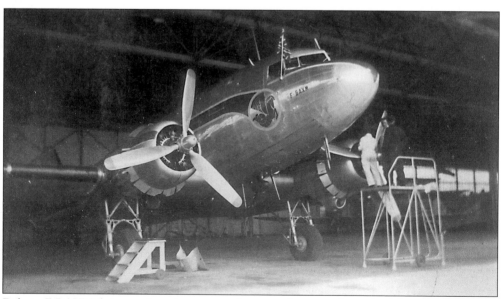

Dakota F-BAXM (note registration repeated on nose) operated on the Manchester to Paris service but on 2 December 1948 suffered magneto drop and had to be taken into the Control Tower Hangar for attention. Both the British Union Flag and French Tricolour are still being flown from the cockpit.

Scottish Airlines Ltd of Prestwick (a quite separate company from the similarly-named Scottish Airways Ltd) operated a large number of Dakotas. In fact their parent company, Scottish Aviation Ltd, was responsible for the civilianization of many ex-military Dakotas from the end of the Second World War. Their Dakota G-AGZG is seen on the apron during 1948 with a Mosquito in the background which had been prepared by Fairey Aviation for export to the Turkish Air Force.

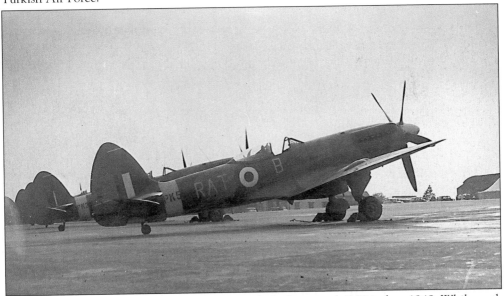

No.613 Squadron replaced their Spitfire 14s with the later mark F.22 in late 1948. While work was being carried out on the runway at Ringway during 1949, the squadron deployed temporarily to the Woodford Aerodrome of A.V. Roe & Co. Ltd. Spitfire coded RAT-B, the unit identifying code when the squadron was in Reserve Command, is with others on the Avro Flight Sheds apron at Woodford, in 1949, which was notorious for its slope.

Four of No.613 Squadron Spitfire FR.14s on the apron of Hangar No.7 in December 1948. The squadron had just been re-equipped with the F.22 version and these aircraft may have been awaiting collection by RAF ferry pilots to be taken to a maintenance unit for scrapping.

On 8 December 1948, Avro Lancaster RE206, due to a misunderstanding between the aircrew and marshallers, collided with the buildings adjoining Hangar No.6, these contained BEA station offices, etc. The aircraft was repaired. In later years this building became the home of the Airport Archive.

Three

The New Terminal Building: 1949

Space was at a premium in the passenger terminal and it was inadequate to deal with the number of passengers now using the airport. Former military buildings, such as Building No.72 which had been designed as the RAF Volunteer Reserve Mess and was later used as a Dining Room and Sergeants Mess for the Parachute Training School, were taken over. Passenger check-in facilities, lounges, a restaurant and a bar were created, along with other services, such as a newspaper and book shop, a branch of a bank and also a machine for purchasing personal accident insurance!

After they checked in, passengers went through the 'gate' and walked along a short passage to the customs area on the east side of the building annexe to Hangar No.6, then to a waiting area, before being conducted across the apron. Another passage, running the length of the rear of the hangar, led to a waiting area for domestic services. A baggage collection area for arrivals was situated behind Hangar No.6, a number of stout metal topped tables were provided!

Arrival of Lord Pakenham, the Minister of Civil Aviation, on 7 February 1949, to formally open the new terminal building. The Lord Mayor of Manchester's Rolls-Royce N10 was the conveyance for the civic celebrations and had an attendant police official.

The official group with: Lord Pakenham; the Lord Mayor of Manchester, Alderman Mary Kingsmill Jones; Councillor Fitzsimons and Councillor Tom Regan.

All passenger baggage had to be checked-in and carefully weighed. Freight was handled separately. The airlines operating into Ringway were responsible for handling passengers and their baggage, with BEA acting for a number of airlines. Three scales are marked for flights operating to Dublin, Belfast and Brussels. BEA Station Clerk George Whitfield awaits passengers in 1949.

The Main Traffic Hall in the terminal building contained the airline passenger-handling desks and a waiting area with, in this case, large comfortable chairs. The intending passengers might have had a long wait in those days!

A restaurant and a bar were created in the new passenger terminal, open to the public as well as passengers and airport staff. They were managed by BEA for many years.

The airport bar was located by the side of the restaurant and Bill Prendergast, the BEA Catering Manager for Ringway, is behind the bar mixing a cocktail. Only a few nationality flags of various airlines 'fly' above the bar at this time.

Visiting on 14 March was the Sud Est Languedoc F-BATJ operated by Air France and positioned in front of Hangar No.6. The three-wheel Esso refueller is noteworthy.

On the apron in front of Hangar No.7 (Royal Auxiliary Air Force) on 18 March 1949 was this RAF Prentice, an aircraft used by many RAF flying schools. The aircraft identity is VS332 and the full code is FC-LY suggesting it came from No.22 Flying Training School at Syerston, in Nottinghamshire, which trained pilots for the Royal Navy. There was a Royal Naval Air Station at Stretton, near Warrington, and the pilot could have been heading for it.

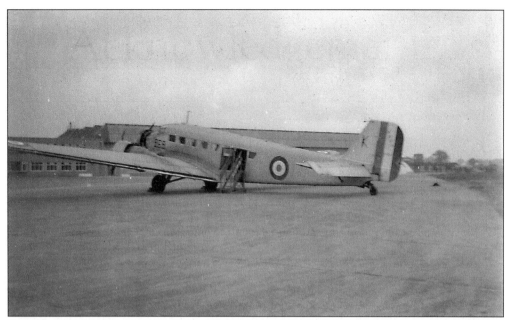

En route from Prestwick to Le Bourget, this French-built AAC 1 (a version of the German Junkers Ju52/3m, from the former Amiot Colombes factory) came into Ringway on 1 April 1949. The aircraft carries the serial or coding 259 below the cockpit and 'K' on the fin. It was noted with the military radio call-sign F-RAUT and belonged to *L'Armee de l'Air*. Parked on the apron in front of Hangar No.6, there is a clear view of Hangar No.7, with the special aerodrome route beacon mounted on this hangar.

Sivewright Airways Miles Aerovan G-AJOI, named *Oldhamia,* in front of the 1938 terminal during 1949. The steps seem to have been 'borrowed' from Air France.

De Havilland Hornet Moth G-ADKK, then used by Bertram Mills Circus, was in the 1938 hangar on 28 May 1949. Sivewright Airways continued to keep their aircraft in this hangar and in the background is their Dakota G-AKSM, named *Bartonia*. It served with the airline for three years.

Beechcraft C.18 Expeditor G-AIYI was operated by David Brown & Co. Ltd and had been fitted out to a VIP standard for Prince Aly Khan. Seen during April, it was later to crash on take-off from Sherburn-in-Elmet aerodrome, near Tadcaster, on 24 August 1949. Evident in the background to Hangar No.6 is the large wartime building erected to house the Dropping Trainer of the Parachute Training School.

KLM DC-4 Skymaster PH-TDL, with a number of other aircraft, was chartered by the Manchester-based Hallé Orchestra on 19 April 1949. A Dutch orchestra had flown in from Amsterdam, and the aircraft returned with the Hallé Orchestra to play in Amsterdam. John Mahieu Aviation Beech Expeditor OO-APD, a regular visitor, is being refuelled on the apron in front of Hangar No.6.

The first KLM Convair 240 to appear at Ringway came on 13 May 1949. PH-TED carried the fleet name *Gerard Terborch*. It was the first pressurized airliner type to use Ringway on a regular basis throughout the year and was used on the Amsterdam service.

Swissair used the DC-4 when necessary. HB-ILO made its first visit on 30 May 1949. The airline, which began services in December the previous year, normally used the Douglas Dakota.

Scottish Airlines Ltd was granted a BEA Associate agreement and in 1949 was flying scheduled passenger services to the Isle of Man. On 3 June 1949 Dragon Rapide G-AKSF was used from Ringway on the service to the Isle of Man via Blackpool. This aircraft was written off at Prestwick, the home base of the airline, less than two months later, on 23 July 1949.

Loading operations required quite a lot of manual work. The BEA Station Engineer Tim Healey, on the extreme left, watches, while BEA Station Superintendent George Absalom is on the right, checking baggage which is loaded on hand trucks. Freight was moved to the aircraft on four-wheel trolleys. The airport porter with the hat stood next to the Shell-BP tanker is Jim Hewitt, whose association with Ringway began in 1938 when he worked for the building contractors, Miskins. A BEA Dakota photographed on 3 August 1949.

George Absalom, the BEA Station Superintendent (seventh from the left), and his staff, which includes a duty officer, load and cargo-control officers, receptionists and Norman Platt, the Senior Traffic Officer, stood to the left of George Abslom. Other staff were manning the telephones!

Customs officer and engineers awaiting Aer Lingus flight crew on a newspaper charter on 14 October 1949. Newspapers, printed in Manchester, were regularly flown to Ireland on special charter flights.

BOAC did not provide services from Ringway, but on 30 December their Dove G-AKCF called *en route* from Prestwick to Filton, Bristol. The type was used for crew training and was normally based at London Airport, Heathrow.

Between 1948 and the end of 1949, Fairey Aviation overhauled a large number of Avro Yorks which were being used on the Berlin Airlift. This RAF York is passing Hangar No.5 heading towards the 1938 terminal area then taxiing onto the Fairey Aviation site some distance away. It had probably landed on Runway 06 and vacated at its threshold, which at the time was in front of Hangar No.6 and the new terminal apron. The prototype Avro York had its first flight at Ringway, on 5 July 1942, and many were built in the hangars on the south side until production was transferred to the Yeadon factory of A.V.Roe & Co. Ltd at what is now Leeds-Bradford Airport.

Fairey Aviation converted this Fairey Firefly SE-BRA to a Target Tug for Svensk Flygtjanst of Stockholm, part of a large contract which, with other military work, kept Fairey Aviation busy during 1949.

Upon the opening of the 1962 terminal, the 1949 terminal (Building No.72) became used for office accommodation. This part of Ringway has now been totally redeveloped but in March 1987 was still used for offices and storage which continued until demolition in 1995 and 1996.

Although the main passenger-handling facilities had moved to the new terminal, the public enclosure by the 1938 terminal remained a popular venue for the citizens of Manchester to watch aircraft at their airport. A commentary on airport movements was broadcast during the summer months by co-author Les Jones. Quite a number of cars can be seen. It would be some years before a 'waving off' enclosure was provided nearer to the scheduled airliner movements. Flags of the various airlines were flown and upper right are the two ticket huts used by the pleasure flying companies. In the distance is the Fairey Aviation site which included their original hangar (the first hangar to be erected on the aerodrome) and the smaller hangars brought over from Barton.

Four

A New Era Begins: 1950-1951

BEA introduced more services in 1950 including one to Paris, which originated at Renfrew Airport, Glasgow, and another beginning at Ringway, calling at Birmingham *en route* to the Channel Islands, Jersey via Guernsey, both using Dakotas.

The main runway was closed in August 1950 to enable an 1,800ft extension and connecting taxi-way to be built at the north-eastern end. It was not until 1952 that Ringway was able to operate on a twenty-four hour basis. Growth in traffic needed better passenger handling, aircraft parking facilities and improved landing aids. A radar-assisted approach system, called Ground Controlled Approach, was brought to Ringway and contained in a series of mobile trailers which were moved depending upon which end of the main runway was in use for landings. In them sat the controllers passing information on height and position to assist the pilot landing his aircraft. The vans in their distinctive orange and white vertical stripes can be seen in the background of a number of photographs.

One of a number of Dragon Rapides converted from RAF Dominies, registered to the Associated Airways Joint Committee, was G-AGSK. It served initially with Channel Island Airways until BEA took over their aircraft and services in 1947. The colour scheme is still silver with basic BEA titling in March 1950 when it called at Ringway. The pilot is wearing the original BEA navy blue uniform whereas BEA duty officer Don Moores wears the new grey uniform.

The Dakota was the stalwart of Aer Lingus's fleet and the company earned extra revenue by carrying freight. In this case Dakota EI-ACH brought in a 22cwt road-roller from Dublin, on 11 April 1950.

Some freight required special attention. Flown into Ringway on 23 May 1950 was a party of seven lion cubs destined for Blackpool. Sabena had brought them from the Belgian Congo and they arrived on their Brussels service.

Fairey Aviation Ltd, having completed a considerable amount of work on de Havilland Mosquitos in previous years, was still involved with some small contracts for further conversions. This unidentified aircraft coded 'G', with a specially modified nose, is thought to be destined for Belgium. Another Mosquito is also on the apron in front of Hangar No.6, on 10 May 1950.

The new fire-engine of the Airport Fire Service shows off its capabilities on a disused, wartime, covered air raid shelter behind the Royal Auxiliary Air Force Hangar No.7.

KLM continued to use their Dakotas but occasionally, when the passenger load required a bigger aircraft, they used the Convair 240 Convairliners. This was the case on 20 June 1950 for the Amsterdam – Manchester – Dublin service.

Pleasure flying was popular from the public enclosure by the 1938 terminal building. This Auster Autocar G-AJYK, being flown by Bruce Martin of Airviews Ltd, was kept very busy in June 1950. The chair, possibly being used as a makeshift step is noteworthy, a practice which would not be permitted today! Unfortunately, the aircraft crashed a few months later, near Leicester, and was written off.

Early production Vickers Vikings needed a modification and were taken out of service, some being stored at Ringway. When the work was completed, the Vikings were sold on to a number of airline companies. Based at Langley Aerodrome was G.S.Sale, trading as Sale & Co., which took G-AGRP, G-AGRV and G-AGRW on charge. One of these aircraft received maintenance in Hangar No.6 and was photographed on 20 July 1950.

This BEA Dakota in Hangar No.6 carries one of the interim colour schemes used by the airline. It had been taken on charge in March from Field Aircraft Services, having been converted to Pionair standard and registered as G-ALXK. No aircraft name is shown but it carries the BEA Flying 'Key' symbol and airline titling between the fuselage stripes instead of above and, interestingly, stripes on the engine nacelles.

Silver City Airways employed a fleet of Bristol 170 Freighters, mainly on charter flights, being well known for their car ferry operations to the Continent from airports in south-east England and also for ferrying British, French and Irish racehorse owners. In November 1950, G-AIME visited (could it have been for the November handicap at the now-closed Manchester Racecourse of Castle Irwell?) on a wet afternoon.

On the morning of 11 December 1950 Aer Lingus Dakota EI-AFC skidded after landing on runway 28 and stopped just short of its western end before the Altrincham to Wilmslow road. It is not too far from the modern-day spectators viewing enclosure! The aircraft was repaired and went on to serve Aer Lingus for the next fourteen years.

This busy apron scene on 16 January 1951 demonstrates the prominence of the Dakota and shows left to right, BEA G-AGIP, Air France F-BAXI, KLM PH-TCT and Swissair HB-IRE, all on the apron before No.6 Hangar.

BEA held a Christmas Party for the children in 1950 and flight steward Tom Angham is casting a watchful eye over the proceedings.

This SNCAC NC702 Martinet, with the aircraft coding 11.S.14, showing it to be of the French Navy (*Aéronavale*), was visiting on 1 March 1951. Over the next few months and years, *Aéronavale* aircraft were no strangers to Ringway since they were used to clear customs when collecting spare parts for the Avro Lancasters in service with *Aéronavale*.

Collection and delivery of small items of freight was done in a van operated by BEA. Driver Len Evans and other members of the handling staff are seen outside the Cargo Office in an annexe to Hangar No.6 on 1 March 1951.

The first conversion to the new Pionair standard was Dakota G-ALYF, appropriately named *Pionair*. However, Pionair Dakota G-AGJW was used for a number of publicity photographs by BEA showing the new insignia including badge in place of the 'Key' symbol and also individual aircraft names. Demonstrated at Ringway on 10 April was G-AGJW, named *Wilfred Park*.

Trans World Charter of Elstree Aerodrome, near London, operated three Vickers Vikings on a world-wide charter basis carrying freight, ship's crews and other passenger charters. Viking G-AHOT was on a charter flight to Lourdes on 18 May 1951 from Ringway. The airline was sold later in the year to Southend-based Crewsair which also operated a number of similar aircraft.

During 1951 Air Navigation & Trading Ltd of Blackpool operated a scheduled service from Blackpool to the Isle of Man under a BEA Associate agreement. De Havilland DH.86B G-ADUF was used by the company on this service but used on a charter from Blackpool to Manchester and on to Belfast on 12 June 1951. This particular aircraft had been built in 1936 for Imperial Airways Ltd, transferring to BOAC and then used in the Middle East during the Second World War. It returned to the UK in 1948. Apron alterations to the concrete at Ringway are evident, as well as work going on in the vicinity of the main runway. An Aer Lingus Dakota is parked on the far side of the apron.

Previous page, Top: The new 'air stairs', one of the improvements carried out to the fleet of BEA Pionairs, with the air hostesses wearing the new style uniforms. The BEA engineer and ground staff are in their current 'uniforms'.
Bottom: BEA station staff at Ringway on 10 April 1951 inspecting the new Pionair standard. Thßey are (from left to right) Station Assistant Johnny Ellis, Station Traffic Officer Norman Platt, Station Clerk ? , Station Assistant Cairns, Station Clerk Maggie Cowan, Flight Clerk McLeish and Station Clerk Janet Milne.

BEA used Hangar No.6 as a maintenance base and was able to carry out major work to the extent of changing engines. Dakota G-AGZB having an engine change on 10 August 1951, the aircraft is still in the old colour scheme and insignia. This aircraft had the distinction, in later years, to have operated the last BEA scheduled Pionair flight out of Heathrow, on 31 October 1960.

The prototype de Havilland Heron G-ALZL was temporarily painted in a number of airline colour schemes, including BEA, to stimulate interest in sales of the type. The aircraft called at Ringway on 15 August 1951 when it wore the latest BEA colour scheme and insignia, one which was to be adopted throughout the BEA fleet. Local BEA management and staff pose in front of the aircraft. Letter 'C' painted on a board above the hut in the background indicates where visiting pilots reported. The Ministry of Civil Aviation operated the Aeronautical Information Service in this hut.

The Aeronautical Information Service maintained full details of controlled airspace, restrictions and danger areas, as well as information on aerodromes and airports. Aircrew could receive the maximum amount of information available to help plan the flight. In the background is Ted Kinnersley, the Briefing Officer, showing a BBC crew of Charles Farmer and Eric Jolley details of restrictions round the Isle of Man, with Captain Geoff Greenhalgh of BEA looking on.

This de Havilland Tiger Moth N6537, coded RCR-K, had been used by No.11 Reserve Flying School based at Scone, in Scotland, until being posted to RAF Ringway Station Flight, hence the retention of its codes still evident on 21 August 1951. It stayed at Ringway for a couple of years until replaced by a de Havilland Canada Chipmunk.

KLM Convair 240 PH-TEG on 21 August 1951. In the background with engines running is a BEA Dakota G-AGYX showing its full registration across the upper surfaces of both wings.

Westland Aircraft Ltd of Yeovil, in Somerset, had obtained the licence to build the American-designed Sikorsky S-51 helicopter in the UK. One of the first to be built by Westland was G-ALIK, which came to Ringway to carry out demonstration flights on 24, 25 and 27 August 1951. In 1955, still used as a company demonstrator, the aircraft was converted to a Westland Widgeon configuration, which had a different nose and rotor head/gearbox.

Above and previous page: During the shipping strike in 1951 airline operators had the opportunity to once again show their capabilities in transporting urgent freight. Silver City Airways was using Bristol 170 Freighter F-BEND (itself on charter from its French owners) and chartered it to Aer Lingus on 18 September 1951 for a flight into Ringway. The ample room and access to the aircraft is well demonstrated, along with the use of fork lift trucks to move freight to and from the aircraft.

Five

Twenty-four Hour Operation Commences: 1952-1958

More direct flights were opened to continental destinations and, in April 1952, BEA recommenced the London service with Vickers Vikings. Towards the end of 1952, Manchester Corporation reached agreement with the Ministry of Civil Aviation that Ringway should remain under the ownership and management of the Corporation. April was also significant in that, on the 29th, the first transatlantic flight from Ringway was undertaken, by a Skyways Avro York G-AHFG whose destination was Kingston, Jamaica. It was not intentional since the aircraft had diverted to Ringway *en route* from London!

The first visit of a turbine-powered aircraft occurred on 20 March 1953, when BEA Viscount G-ALWE, named *Discovery*, arrived on a demonstration flight. It was to be another twelve months before regular services were introduced by BEA and Aer Lingus on 11 April 1954, with Air France following in July. Positioned on 28 October 1953 was Sabena Douglas DC-6B OO-CTH. This aircraft introduced the first scheduled transatlantic service from New York to Manchester then Brussels on 30 October 1953. In the following year BOAC began their Atlantic service using Boeing Stratocruisers. Long distance international flights had started even though they were not direct, as intermediary stops had to be made to take on fuel.

Airwork took over the central south side hangar (No.522) in April 1954 to overhaul North American Sabre fighters of the Royal Canadian Air Force (later including Royal Air Force Sabres), a contract shared with their facilities at nearby Speke Airport, Liverpool.

Ringway was still known by its original title of Manchester (Ringway) Airport but, in June 1954, this was changed to Manchester Airport. In 1955 it was decided that an entirely new terminal building and apron area were necessary.

The first licensed Inclusive Tour flight was operated on 29 May 1955 by an Air Kruise (Kent) Ltd Dakota G-AMYV to Ostend, which took a party to pick up a coach for a tour of Europe. These charters were flown for a number of tour companies. Lufthansa began the first scheduled service to Canada on 23 April 1956 with Lockheed Super Constellations from Hamburg, Dusseldorf, then Manchester, and on to Shannon, in the Republic of Ireland, for refuelling, then Montreal, ending at Chicago, in the United States. The summer of 1956 saw a British Eagle Vickers Viscount service from Liverpool to Manchester, then Ostend.

Ringway was becoming an aircraft engineering centre. In April 1956 BEA started carrying out Check 1 maintenance on Viscounts to allow greater flexibility in the positioning of the fleet. Hangar No.6 had been used for overnight maintenance but the introduction of the Viscount created a little problem, the tail was too high to get the complete aircraft into the hangar. Fitted onto the hangar floor was a ramp to lift the nose as the aircraft moved forward, thereby dropping the tail so that it could pass under the roof overhang safely. The interior of the hangar was adequate for the height of the tail. Late in 1958 BEA took over the Fairey Hangar No.5A to service Viscounts and that also became the home of the BAC1-11 fleet.

It was in early 1957 that No.613 Squadron and 1951 AOP Flight ceased flying, both units being disbanded by the end of March. On 28 January 1966 a memorial to No.613 Squadron was unveiled in the new terminal building and a further memorial on a plinth was dedicated outside the Terminal One building in January 2000. Work started on the new terminal foundations in October 1957. Fortunately, the work area was well away from the operational area but it was eventually to lead to the closure of Yewtree Lane and meant a much greater distance to travel along other roads to the Fairey Aviation site.

Another extension to the main runway 06/24 was opened on 23 April 1958, bringing the operational length from 5,900ft to 7,000ft, enabling larger aircraft to operate more safely when fully loaded. BOAC returned, having used the American base at Burtonwood, near Warrington, on a temporary basis. The radio landing aid, Standard Beam Approach System, installed shortly after the end of the Second World War, was replaced by the new American-designed Instrument Landing System, a much more modern type of equipment.

Ringway had known the operation of jet-powered aircraft since No.613 Squadron Royal Auxiliary Air Force had re-equipped with the de Havilland Vampire but it was not until 30 July 1958 that a pure-jet airliner came to Ringway. Air France brought the Sud Caravelle F-BHHI on a demonstration flight. The type was introduced on the Paris-Manchester route on 1 June 1961.

Overseas Air Transport (Jersey) Ltd made Ringway its base and became known as Mercury Airlines Ltd, operating scheduled services with de Havilland Herons from Ringway and other airports, including some flights for other airlines. A Dakota was used in 1964, newspaper flights being a useful source of revenue. At the end of 1964 flying ceased and the company was taken over by British Midland Airways Ltd which enabled that airline to obtain more facilities at Ringway.

Aer Lingus, pushing ahead with its plans to expand its activities, had promoted a freight service to Dublin and ordered a number of improved Bristol Freighters known as Wayfarers. The company leased and registered EI-AFP from the manufacturers, who had previously used it as a trials aircraft. A variety of loads were carried and on 23 June 1952 it was being unloaded of bales of cloth for the Bradford Dyers Association. BEA engineers are in attendance.

Air France operated a service to Dinard, using Douglas DC-4 F-BBDA, named *Ciel de Bretagne*, on 5 July 1952. The aircraft is taking on fuel from the Shell-BP tankers and in the background contractors' vehicles are seen on the main runway finishing off work which had begun in 1950.

KLM standardized with the Convair 240 on the Amsterdam – Ringway – Dublin service in 1952, followed by a later version, the 340, until 1957, when Vickers Viscounts were introduced. Convairliner PH-TEC taking off and viewed from the south side showing the Fairey Aviation hangars on 20 August 1952. The large hangar to the right, appearing below the Convair 240, was demolished to make way for the new Monarch hangar in 1995.

BEA carefully documented their own flights and also flights of other airlines where they had an operations agreement, with this work being carried out in Flight Operations (Ship's Papers). The 'office' was contained in one of the huts overlooking the apron close to the AIS Briefing Hut, Meteorological Service Hut and the small Marshaller's Hut. A telephone system was the main line of communication, especially with other BEA stations.

De Havilland Vampire FB.5 VZ267 wears the codes allocated to No.613 Squadron, Royal Auxiliary Air Force and individual aircraft letter 'L'. Originally, the codes were carried on the nose but were moved to the booms, aircraft being painted silver overall with the British nationality markings. This photograph is thought to have been taken during the winter of 1952-1953, since by late 1953 the squadron aircraft had received camouflage and unit codes were replaced by squadron markings.

No.613 Squadron Vampires lined up outside Hangar No.7, with the two Meteor T.7 aircraft at the far end near to the civil apron in front of Hangar No.6. The squadron aircraft, with the exception of the Meteors, had now received their grey-green upper surface and silver under-surface camouflage with the squadron colour bars green/yellow/green on each side of the roundel.

Auster J/1 Autocrat G-AGYP of the Ringway Aero Club during 1953. It had a pale yellow and green colour scheme and was fitted with blind-flying instruments and a long-range fuel tank which can be seen under the aircraft. The concrete apron with its skimming of tarmacadam to tone it down, a relic of the war, is still evident.

The Ringway Aero Club obtained the services of Mrs Gabrielle Patterson as an instructor on a voluntary basis. Previously she had been an instructor at the Lancashire Aero Club at Barton Aerodrome and also the South Staffordshire Flying Club at Walsall. Mrs Patterson was the first woman to be appointed to the Guild of Air Pilots and Navigators panel of examiners and also flew during the Second World War with the Air Transport Auxiliary. In this photograph, taken during 1953, she is discussing a trial lesson with Mr N.Cairns, a BEA duty officer. Auster J/1 Autocrat G-AGYP is in the background.

Sabena continued to use the Dakota on their Brussels service until April 1953 but they were still regularly seen for some years afterwards. This is OO-AUV, shown here on 17 June 1953.

Dragon Rapide G-AGDM, operated by Airviews Ltd, was a familiar sight at Ringway between 1951 and 1957. It was regularly flown by Bruce Martin and must have given the first experience of flight to many Mancunians, as well as being used on charter flights and scheduled services to the Channel Islands (via Southampton) and the Isle of Man, both popular routes. The aircraft itself was delivered to Allied Airways (Gandar Dower) Ltd at Dyce Aerodrome, Aberdeen, in 1941 for Scottish services not controlled by the Associated Airways Joint Committee. After the war, it was taken over by BEA, then Sivewright Airways Ltd, and finally, when that airline ceased operations, by Airviews Ltd.

BOAC inaugurated their transatlantic service from Ringway with flights starting at London Heathrow, then Manchester, Prestwick, and on to New York, with Boeing Stratocruisers. The first service was on 7 May 1954 with G-ALSC, named *Centaurus*. For a short period BOAC transferred the Manchester stop to the American Air Base at Burtonwood, near Warrington, which had a longer runway and was safer when taking off with a more heavily-loaded aircraft.

BOAC Stratocruiser G-ALSC departing Manchester, for New York, on the first service on 7 May 1954. Noticeable are the black and white runway marker boards and also the central hangar of the south side, which was demolished with two others to make way for the second runway works.

Air India International did a demonstration flight to Ringway on 26 July 1954 using Lockheed L-1049C Super Constellation VT-DGM. It was in Europe for fitting a new galley by KLM at Amsterdam, being delivered to the airline at the end of the month.

Scottish Aviation Ltd, of Prestwick Airport, in Scotland, developed their Twin Pioneer rugged transport aircraft and embarked on a sales tour. One of the development aircraft is seen here on the apron in front of No.6 Hangar in 1954. The nose markings are interesting in that many aircraft of the day carried elaborate insignia. The aircraft could be the prototype G-ANTP.

Fairey Aviation began assembling the Fairey Gannet Anti-Submarine aircraft in 1954 at Ringway, for the Royal Navy and Royal Australian Navy. The aircraft were built at the Heaton Chapel, Stockport, factory and some 100 aircraft were completed. This aircraft, WN447, is parked outside the original Fairey hangar by Yewtree Lane. The area is now where the FLS Aerospace hangar stands. In the background can be seen a line-up of Douglas Invaders of the United States Air Force, Fairey Aviation had received a contract to overhaul a large number of these aircraft.

Swissair also used the CV.240 on the service to Zurich, and HB-IRV is on the main runway 06/26, just by the intersection with runway 02/20, on 6 May 1955. The type was replaced by a later version, the 440, in 1957. USAF B-26s at Faireys, in the background.

Dragon Airways Ltd obtained a licence to fly seasonal scheduled services from a number of local airports, which included Liverpool (Speke) Airport, and Stoke-on-Trent (Meir) Airport, (now closed) as well as Ringway, using the Dragon Rapide. In 1955, the de Havilland Heron replaced the Rapide and the company took over some Hunting-Clan routes, especially Newcastle. This Heron, a Mark 1b with fixed undercarriage, is at Ringway on 30 May 1955, just as the airline took delivery of the aircraft.

This piture of BEA Pioneer Dakota G-ALLI on 4 July 1955 has added interest in that parked in front of Hangar No.523 south side, in the background, are a number of Canadair-built Sabres and Lockheed T-33 Silver Stars. After service with the Royal Canadian Air Force in Europe, they were destined for NATO countries, such as Greece and Turkey, following overhaul by Airwork Ltd at Ringway.

The Dragon Rapide still remained in use by a number of charter operators. G-ALBA was used by Ringway Air Charter Services Ltd but, by the end of 1955, had been taken over by Airviews Ltd. The hangar in the background (a Bellman), erected prior to the Second World War, was used by A.V. Roe & Co. Ltd, at one time housing the Avro Manchester bomber prototypes.

No.2 Hangar, adjacent to the 1938 control tower and terminal, was used to house a number of light aircraft and the fleet of Airviews Ltd. Pictured on 11 June 1955 is the Miles Sparrowjet G-ADNL which was normally based at Barton and used on occasions for air-racing by Fred Dunkerley. In 1957, he was to win the King's Cup in this aircraft, at a speed of 228mph. Also in the photograph is Auster Autocar G-AOBV, just registered to Basil de Ferranti, to be used for charter work and pleasure flights at Ringway by North West Air Services.

The main apron in front of No.6 Hangar was becoming cramped and the decision was taken in 1954 to demolish one of the temporary wartime hangars and build an extension to the apron. A new spectators or 'waving-off' enclosure was also created between the new apron and the car park. The area is now roughly where Pier A of Terminal One is built with all its extensions. Hunting-Clan operated a feeder service from Ringway to Newcastle, where they operated flights to Scandinavia. Dakota G-AMSK is shown here, probably on 22 June 1955, just before Hunting-Clan handed over the service to Dragon Airways.

Owned by Platts (Barton) Ltd as an executive transport, this Airspeed Consul G-AHEG was a familiar aircraft at Ringway. It is seen here on 27 July 1955 in front of the control tower. In the background is an Aer Lingus Dakota parked on one of the wartime 'frying pan' hard stands off the main airline apron.

Fairey Aviation overhauled some sixty Douglas B-26 Invaders for the United States Air Force. Seen here in April 1956 is serial 435790. The aircraft were lined up alongside Hangar No.4 of the Fairey site. This aircraft was painted black with red individual markings but the fin and rudder of 435779 carries yellow chevrons.

Douglas RB-26C Invader seen outside Fairey Hangar No.4 in April 1956. The hangar still shows signs of its wartime camouflage and, unlike many of the wartime hangars erected at Ringway, still survives in use to house aircraft.

Lufthansa opened the first schedule service from Ringway to Canada, with Lockheed L-1049G Super Constellations, on 23 April 1956. The aircraft came from Hamburg and Dusseldorf, calling at Ringway, and then to Shannon, for refuelling, and on to Montreal, completing the service at Chicago, in the United States. Runway limitations caused the service to cease at the end of the year but it was reinstated in 1959. Super Constellation D-ALOP is seen here in September 1956 on the apron in front of No.6 Hangar.

The Ministry of Transport and Civil Aviation operated the Civil Aviation Flying Unit based at Stansted Airport, in Essex. Their small fleet of Percival Princes carried special equipment to monitor airfield radio, radar and navigational aids. This Prince G-AMKY visited Ringway on several occasions and is seen here, probably early in 1957, wearing the British Civil Air Ensign on the fin.

Eagle Aviation took over the larger part of No.2 Hangar for engineering operations, principally rebuilding Dakotas, the first of which arrived by road in March 1956 It became G-AOJI the following year. It is in the background, nearly complete, probably in September 1956. The Airspeed Oxford in the foreground formerly served with the Belgian Air Force and was registered in the UK as G-AOUT, to be used ultimately for spares recovery and was then dismantled. Eagle moved to the south side central hangar (No.522) when it was vacated by Airwork.

Aer Lingus operated their bare metal Dakotas from Dublin to the UK, regularly flying through an industrialized atmosphere which tended to make the aircraft look more than a little dirty. The decision was taken to repaint the aircraft, the first being noted at Ringway early in 1956. Dakota EI-ACK, named *St Albert*, is seen on the apron extension awaiting passengers in September 1956.

No.613 Squadron Vampires being refuelled one Saturday morning in 1956.

Like all the flying units of the Royal Auxiliary Air Force, No.613 Squadron was disbanded on 10 March 1957. The whole squadron posed for this photograph on Sunday 20 January 1957, the news of the forthcoming disbandment having been announced earlier in the month. Within the next few months everything had gone and RAF Station Ringway closed down about twelve months later.

Sabena began operating the Douglas DC-7C after withdrawal of the DC-6B on the service to New York. This aircraft, OO-CFF, was actually registered in the Belgian Congo. It is parked in front of Hangar No.6 on 4 May 1957. Baggage handling was still very much on a manual basis, and a bicycle seems to be the prime method of transporting staff!

The standard aircraft operating between provincial airports was the Dakota. There were always a couple of BEA Pionair Dakotas parked at Ringway and this one was in a regular position near to the Fire Station on 11 May 1957. The Dakota was being phased out of service with BEA, most having gone by the end of 1961.

Pleasure flying continued to be provided by two companies at Ringway, located by the 1938 terminal building. Auster Autocar G-AOBV could take three passengers and was flown regularly by Harry Patterson of North West Air Services, also for charter for aerial photography. The flight often involved a take off from nearby runway 20, heading south then a turn east to fly north over the Gatley/Heald Green area to land from the north-east on runway 24, or a slightly extended flight to land on runway 20, then back to the flight ticket hut in the enclosure.

Harry Patterson bought G-AOJH, a Canadian-built de Havilland Fox Moth. Exported from Canada to Pakistan, it was then imported into the UK. Its first visit to Ringway was on the back of a wagon *en route* to Sherburn-in-Elmet aerodrome, where it was to be brought up to airworthiness standard. Summer pleasure flights and charter work commenced at Manchester Airport, in March 1958, from the public enclosure by the 1938 terminal in the background. The aircraft later moved to Speke Airport, Liverpool, as its operational base.

Airviews Ltd took delivery of Dragon Rapide G-AFRK in May 1956, along with G-AGSH, up to this time both aircraft had served with BEA. A number of Dragon Rapides were used by Airviews on scheduled services to the Isle of Wight, via Southampton, and other destinations. Taking fuel on from a three-wheel tanker on the 1938 terminal apron, where Airviews normally operated their aircraft, is G-AFRK in 1958. The following year this aircraft was withdrawn from use.

Many local organizations chartered aircraft for business trips to the Continent at this time. The local branch of the Spar Grocery chain of independent shops used this Derby Airways Dakota to spend a few days in Amsterdam visiting their continental counterparts.

Jersey Airlines Ltd obtained its first de Havilland Heron in 1953, the first British airline to operate the type. A fleet of them was used on services radiating from the Channel Islands, to England, Wales, and the Continent, with G-AMYU being the first aircraft used. They were seen regularly on services from Ringway to southern England and the Channel Islands, with G-AMYU at Ringway on 20 June 1958. The company was absorbed by the British United Airways group in 1962.

Independent Air Travel Ltd was formed in 1956 with Vickers Vikings. It mainly operated charter and Inclusive Tour services from airports in southern England. Contracts were secured with tour operators in the north of England for 1958. Viking G-AHPG came into Ringway on 20 July 1958 to operate such a flight.

Occasionally, Air France operated one of their L-749 Constellations into Ringway, with F-BAZJ shown here on 16 June 1958. The famous Jackson's brickworks chimney is in the background. This actual aircraft had been used in 1951 by the President of France on a visit to the United States. After service with Air France it was delivered to the military *Armée de l'Air* and converted to an airborne Search and Rescue aircraft.

Six
Major Rebuilding:
1959-1962

Work had started on the new terminal with the control tower/administration block being completed first of all and opened to Air Traffic Control in April 1961. The 1938 terminal building/hangar and temporary hangars had to be demolished to make way for the new apron.

Sabena replaced the DC-7C with the Boeing 707 on the New York service on 20 April 1960. In July BEA Vickers Vanguard G-APED made a series of route-proving trials calling at Ringway, but the first regular scheduled service using this type did not start until 1 November 1961. The first jet service to Europe was opened on 1 July 1961 by Air France, using the Sud Aviation Caravelle.

Aer Lingus replaced the Dakotas with the Fokker F.27 Friendship on the service Dublin – Manchester – Amsterdam from April 1957. EI-AKG, delivered in the middle of 1959, is on the former RAF apron, used as an overflow to the main apron. It would leave the passengers a short walk to the International arrival gate by Hangar No.6.

Swissair introduced a scheduled cargo flight to New York in 1955 using Douglas DC-4s but brought into service the DC-6A (Cargo) which had a greater capacity. HB-IBB was on the service at Ringway on 10 May 1959.

Federated Air Transport Ltd was based at Liverpool (Speke) Airport and operated charters for its owner, a fruit and vegetable wholesaler in Liverpool. Dragon Rapide G-ANZP is at Ringway on 16 May 1959. Some weeks later it was used by Captain Harry Patterson of North West Air Services, based at Ringway, on a charter to Nottingham (Tollerton) Aerodrome.

BOAC, having suspended Atlantic flights from Ringway, returned with the Douglas DC-7C. Their *Seven Seas* G-AOIH is taking off from runway 24 on 18 May 1959.

Fairey Aviation commenced production of Firefly drones to be used as unmanned aircraft in guided missile training. A number of surplus Fireflies were converted to the U.9 configuration. WB416 is shown here on Fairey's apron on 12 June 1959. The distinctive colour scheme was yellow upper surfaces with red under surfaces and British nationality markings. Many of the aircraft were flown (with pilot, as no unmanned flights were undertaken at Ringway) to the Royal Naval Air Station at nearby Stretton, south of Warrington, for allocation to the unit operating Fireflies for use over the north Wales and Malta firing ranges.

Sabena replaced their Convair 240s with the later version 440, known as the Metropolitan. On 21 September 1959 OO-SCO arrived at Ringway. The type remained on the Brussels service until 1964 when it was replaced with Sud Caravelles.

Dan-Air Services Ltd operated many charter flights through Ringway, especially in later years when their fleet of de Havilland Comets became well known. They also wanted to develop freight charters and had a small fleet of Bristol Freighters. G-APLH was also used for passenger charters and parked in front of the 1938 terminal in 1959.

Closure of the USAF base at Burtonwood, near Warrington, meant a number of troop and family flights using Ringway in 1958 and 1959. Many of these flights were by chartered American civil airliners but a number of military aircraft also came into Ringway, sometimes as a diversion from Burtonwood. Douglas C-124C Globemaster, serial 30044, seen in late 1959, was perhaps one of the largest aircraft to operate into Ringway at the time.

Anonymous-looking Dragon Rapide G-APBM was owned and operated by Air Couriers (Transport) Ltd, a company based at Croydon Airport, until its closure during 1959. Their aircraft were seen regularly at British airports, including Ringway. G.APBN is seen here at Ringway on 3 October 1959. This Rapide had seen previous service with the Royal Netherlands Air Force.

Two German-registered North America Harvards, D-FDOK and D-FGAL, called at Ringway for half an hour on 3 October 1959 . They were specially equipped with smoke generators for sky-writing, although it is not known if they performed over Manchester!

Overseas Air Transport (Jersey) Ltd operated a number of Herons from 1959 and set up its base at Ringway early in 1960. The first visit of G-AOZN was on 6 February 1960, prior to a freight service carrying newspapers to the Isle of Man the next day. Outer engines are being run on the apron in front of the control tower hangar. The Ministry Commer van in its black and yellow scheme, pre-war Bellman hangar used by Avro, Airviews Ltd/Airviews (Manchester) Ltd hut and the Airport Fire Station are noteworthy. The following year Overseas began operating as Mercury Airlines Ltd.

A cluttered scene showing Vickers Viscount G-APKF on the apron by the Ministry of Transport and Civil Aviation Aeronautical Information Service briefing hut. A large number of trolleys and handling equipment were now being used and this corner, by the main vehicle access to the apron, must have caused some problem from time to time. In those days, there was no physical barrier to the apron, security problems being rare.

Heron G-AOXL had the distinction of being one of the last commercial aircraft to fly out of Croydon Airport before its closure in 1959. Morton Air Services Ltd moved to Gatwick Airport and included Ringway in its network of charter services, with G-AOXL shown here at Ringway on 25 May 1960.

An unidentified Viscount wearing the new BEA colour scheme on the main apron while Captain Tommy Charters and Flight Officer Lambert, in their summer uniforms, pose for the camera.

A BEA Viscount in its new colour scheme, with an Aer Lingus Viscount and an Air France Caravelle. International flights requiring customs clearance went to the far annexe where the Caravelle is positioned – a place which Air France Dakotas had occupied in earlier years. The Volkswagen van seems to be a new form of crew bus. There was usually a police presence on the apron.

Fred Olsen Lines, of Norway, often used Ringway to position ship's crews and Curtis Commando LN-FOS, a type not often seen at Ringway, was parked in front of the 1938 terminal. The public enclosure and Yewtree Lane remain, but not for long.

BEA acquired a Mini-van to help their Traffic Branch move documents, etc. to aircraft on the apron. This Viscount G-AMOB, named *William Baffin*, has arrived with passengers carrying 'goodie bags' indicating that they had gone through duty-free at the airport of departure rather than in internal flight. The steps carry the new BEA logo.

Gordon Erridge (left), who was the BEA Manager for England and Wales, based in Manchester, greeting BEA board member Sir Giles Guthrie by the Domestic Arrivals annexe alongside Hangar No.6. Sir Giles Guthrie, who was appointed to the BEA board in 1959, took over as BOAC Chairman and Chief Executive on 1 January 1964. With C.W.A.Scott he won the Schlesinger England to Johannesburg air race in 1936, in Percival Vega Gull G-AEKE, the only aircraft to finish the race. Gordon Erridge retired from BEA in 1967 having served as manager since 1948.

The new BEA colour scheme restricted the aircraft registration letters to the tip of the fin, very difficult to read from a distance! The apron is already being improved, roughly where the huts stood next to Hangar No.6.

Dan-Air Avro York G-ANTI landing on runway 24 on 7 June 1960. The new control tower is under construction and a Jersey Airlines Heron is awaiting line-up for take off on runway 24. The hangar in the background is No.7 which was used by the Royal Auxiliary Air Force until 1957.

Eagle Airways Ltd had used Ringway as an Engineering base and, in common with a number of other charter firms, provided a service for the Inclusive Tour operators. Vickers Viking G-AIHA, carrying their fleet name *Sir Richard Kempenfelt*, is shown on 4 August 1960. Within a few months the aircraft was withdrawn from use. The aircraft was probably one of the few Vikings on the British civil register which had not served with BEA, as it was used by Vickers-Armstrong as a company demonstrator, then by Central African Airways for ten years, before being acquired by Eagle.

Sabena, one of the Atlantic pioneers from Manchester, launched the Boeing 707 on its New York service on 1 June 1960 – the first scheduled jetliner service from Ringway. Their aircraft OO-SJB is seen taxiing on runway 06 on 22 October 1960.

Vickers Vanguard G-APED, named *Defiance*, was used on a number of route-proving flights before the type entered service with BEA late in 1960, with flights mainly out of London. It visited Ringway on such a flight from Hanover. Vanguards were used on scheduled services from 1 November 1961.

BEA Station Superintendent 'Tommy' Adams meeting Captain N. Barker who had brought the first Vanguard G-APED to Ringway in 1960.

Armstrong Whitworth Argosy G-APRN visited Ringway in 1960 wearing its manufacturer's livery and full name. Armstrong Whitworth lost its separate identity within the Hawker Siddeley Group in 1961. Later the aircraft saw service with BEA on freight services.

Dan-Air Avro York G-ANTI on the apron by the side of the Bellman Hangar No.4 which tended to be used as a garage for the airport vehicles. Freight is being loaded on 2 June 1961.

Lufthansa recommenced their flights into Ringway on 3 April 1959 and later introduced the L-1649 Starliner. D-ALAN is seen taking off on runway 24 on 5 August 1961. Faireys is in the background with the Gloster Meteor, probably VT340 which they had used in connection with the Fireflash guided missile trials.

BOAC Boeing 707 G-APFJ, delivered to the company in September 1960, is taxiing to the end of runway 24 with BEA Viscount G-AMOB, still in its old colour scheme, helping to frame the view. The 707 was preserved and is on exhibition in the British Airways collection at the RAF Museum, Cosford.

A number of Italian-built Piaggio P.166 executive transports were imported into the UK from 1960. They were bought by large concerns, including steel companies and breweries, as executive transports. United Steel's G-APVE was resident at Ringway and normally hangared on the south side. It is seen here in 1961.

Skyways of London Ltd obtained a number of ex-BOAC Lockheed L-749 Constellations in 1959 to use on charter services, including G-ANUR, at Ringway in the 'overnight bay', on 6 June 1962. The company was taken over by Euravia (London) Ltd, which became Britannia Airways in 1964.

Falcon Airways Ltd started operations in 1959 doing charter work for the Inclusive Tour market. Their fleet included a number of ex-BOAC Handley Page Hermes IV aircraft. G-ALDA is receiving attention in a central south side hangar on 17 June 1960.

Another ex-BOAC Handley Page Hermes IV, G-ALDI on 12 August 1962. The type was withdrawn from service later in the year. Silver City Airways Ltd became a member of the British United Airways Ltd group. The new control tower and terminal building, visible in the background, are nearing completion.

The 1938 hangar and control tower remain in this 1960 photograph, taken from the edge of the apron in front of Hangar No.6. The two Bellman hangars, huts and the old farm buildings have gone and Yewtree Lane is closed to public access. The framework of the new terminal is rising on foundations laid the previous year.

The new control tower/administration block was the first building to be completed on the new site, as it was intended to bring Air Traffic Control into use as quickly as possible so the 1938 buildings could be demolished. Air Traffic Control moved in April 1961.

A good view from the edge of the apron by Hangar No.6 of progress. RAF de Havilland Comet C.2 XK716, named *Cepheus*, of No.216 Squadron is being refuelled. This particular Comet had been built in the de Havilland factory at nearby Chester. The Ministry huts still remained but were soon to be demolished. Hangar No.6 was not demolished until 1996 when the area was required for the development of Terminal Three.

The control tower and administration block virtually complete. The name *Manchester* is prominent on the blue cladding, which in later years was changed to black, when the new administration block was built to the rear.

This is the new Traffic Hall nearing external completion, *c.*1962. Noteworthy is the expanse of open land to the rear, now covered by further airport development. The hall still remains but has been considerably altered and swallowed up by developments.

The public land-side entrance to the terminal building had an imposing frontage including a decorative frieze. The approach road is being prepared and most of the building appears to be externally complete, dating the photograph to 1962.

This photograph, taken from the new control tower, probably late in 1962 judging by the 'cleaned up' look, shows the Shell-BP and Esso fuel installations. These buildings had in fact been the first to be erected on the new site. In the background are the buildings of the former RAF Station which the airport had taken over when vacated in 1957. The high, pitched-roof building, the former drill hall, came to be used by the Airport Sports and Social Club, the Officers Mess, immediately behind it, was taken over for office use and is one of the few buildings to survive at the present time. The former Station Headquarters had already been taken over by the airport management as offices by the early 1950s. Over on the right is the former Royal Auxiliary Air Force Hangar No.7, the beacon on the roof was out of use but rescued for preservation when this hangar was demolished.

Seven

Ringway 'Takes Off': 1962-1970

The new terminal building was officially opened by HRH Prince Philip, the Duke of Edinburgh, on 22 October 1962, being brought into public use on 3 December 1962. It had all the modern facilities, especially viewing terraces for the public. Airways radar moved into the tower block in March 1963, making Ringway an important centre, not only for airline operations, but for the safe control of aircraft flying in the region.

One of the longest-serving companies at Ringway is Northern Executive Aviation Ltd, founded in late 1961, with delivery of their first aircraft, a Piper Cherokee G-ARVS, in April 1962. Their fleet has been increased to cope with the growth in air taxi work. The company is now one of the country's leading air taxi and charter operators.

BOAC introduced their Boeing 707s in April 1963, the first BOAC transatlantic flight to originate in Manchester. These were replaced in Spring 1966 when BOAC launched the Vickers Super VC.10 on transatlantic flights and the first scheduled non-stop jet service from Manchester to New York on 29 April 1969.

It was in 1965 that the BAC 1-11 made its mark at Ringway. The first visit of the type was on 8 January. British United Airways brought in G-ASJC, they were the first airline to order the type. Aer Lingus had also ordered the 1-11 and used EI-ANE on a proving flight on 27 May 1965. The 1-11 replaced the Viscount on the service to Frankfurt.

BEA introduced the Hawker Siddeley Trident 1 on their service to Paris, in place of the Viscount, on 1 July 1965. Scandinavian Airlines started their first scheduled service, from Copenhagen – Manchester – Dublin, with Caravelle SE-DAC on 1 April 1966. The first visit of a Boeing 737 of Britannia Airways occurred on 27 August 1968 with G-AVRM used on crew training, these aircraft becoming a familiar sight in the following years.

Many of the new airlines operating into Ringway needed ground engineers and staff to assist with the handling of passengers. Servisair Ltd became established at Ringway in 1967, with their passenger steps to aircraft and vehicles often seen on the apron. They continue to provide a similar service on the modern airport.

Extensions of the main runway began, followed by major work bridging the A538 road. The new road tunnel was opened on 15 November 1968 and the extension of the main runway on 7 January 1969. The width of the runway was increased to 200ft and a small extension was made to the north-east by the following August to give a full length of 9,200ft.

Plans were formulated in 1969 to cater for the growing number of passengers and to build a new pier ('C'), aprons and taxiways, extend the traffic hall and build a multi-storey car park, which were completed in 1974. A new fire station was opened on 8 January 1970. An extension to the domestic passenger wing was completed that year, which saw the first visit of a Boeing 747.

The next thirty years saw a tremendous growth in air traffic and the variety of airlines using the airport. The 1962 terminal piers have developed into 'mini' terminals while a new terminal opened giving rise to renaming as Terminal One and the new one as Terminal Two to handle long distance flights. A new terminal (Three) was created alongside Terminal One for British Airways operations . Hotel and office accommodation has increased and a railway station has been built so the catchment area of Manchester Airport is greatly extended. A new 'Second Runway' has been completed and there are plans to extend accommodation and passenger handling to meet demand.

HRH Prince Philip, the Duke of Edinburgh, being shown round the new terminal by Airport Director George Harvey, on 22 October 1962, shortly after the formal opening. Police are in close attendance and in the background can be seen the new Traffic Hall.

The Queen's Flight Heron XH375 is seen awaiting the Royal party by Gate 22 on the Domestic Pier. A quite empty scene, soon to be filled after the terminal came into full use on 3 December 1962.

HRH Prince Philip, the Duke of Edinburgh, departing through Gate 22.

HRH Prince Philip, the Duke of Edinburgh, thanking an official party of VIPs including the Lord Mayor of Manchester, Alderman R.E. Thomas.

The first aircraft operated by Northern Executive Aviation was a Piper Cherokee G-ARVS and the company moved its base to Ringway in 1962. In addition to charter work and aerial photography, it was used on joy-riding flights from a special area adjacent to the main entrance of the spectator terraces in the new terminal.

NEA had moved its headquarters over to the south side when the old 1938 terminal and hangar was demolished. They took over a section of Hangar No.522 erecting a hut at the rear. Boys and girls of Holden Lane Junior High School, Stoke-on-Trent, were given an educational visit and shown over the Piper Cherokee.

Mercury Heron G-AOZN on approach to land on 20 February 1963. Mercury Airlines Ltd operated scheduled services with de Havilland Herons from Ringway and other airports, including some flights for other airlines.

Derby Airways Ltd opened a new service from Manchester to Ostend on 25 May 1963. Canadair C-4 Argonaut G-ALHY is loading passengers on 29 June 1963 from the International Pier. This view of the terminal building and the then Domestic Pier is now almost unrecognizable because of major developments to improve the airport terminal. To reflect the wider operations of Derby Airways, it was renamed British Midland in 1964.

One of the Vickers Vikings originally registered to Airwork Ltd in 1947, it served in the Middle East before being acquired by Tradair Ltd, then with Channel Airways as G-AJFR. At Ringway on 1 June 1964, the aircraft was taken out of service by the end of 1964, but was stored for a few years before being broken up.

British Eagle leased this Vickers Viscount G-AMOC between 1964 and 1965, from Channel Airways, for the holiday routes from Ringway to Nice, and several Inclusive Tour destinations. It was used on 21 June 1964, the apron looks very tidy and by runway 06/24 are the Ground Controlled Approach vehicles.

Adria Airways operated Inclusive Tour flights to Yugoslavia, and Douglas DC-6B YU-AFC was a regular visitor to Ringway. It awaits passengers on the International Pier, some baggage is already on trolleys. The area behind the aircraft is now covered by the new Pier 'C' and aprons of Terminal Two. It was photographed on 21 June 1964.

British Eagle Britannia G-AOVE taxiing out on 21 June 1964. The aircraft had seen previous service with BOAC and had just been delivered to British Eagle. At about this time, the company unsuccessfully applied for a scheduled service licence to be granted on the Manchester to London route.

BOAC introduced their Boeing 707s in April 1963 on transatlantic flights originating in Manchester. On 21 June 1964 the 707 G-ARRA was alongside International Pier B and about to leave, approximately in the position where the present day Stand No.4 is located.

This Vickers Viking was built for the then King's Flight and served with the RAF until bought by the Southend company Tradair Ltd to increase their fleet of Vikings. Channel Airways Ltd took over Tradair in 1962 and used it on flights into Ringway, including here on 21 June 1964. The land behind the apron was later developed but just discernable is the crossbar and lead-in lights which were temporarily installed on runway 20, replacing a short set of approach lights. A radar head is seen in the distance.

Arriving is Handley Page Dart-Herald G-APWG of British United (Channel Islands) Airways Ltd on 21 June 1964. The colour schemes in those days were not as flamboyant as some seen in present times!

Vickers Vanguard G-APEE of BEA on the Domestic Pier on 21 June 1964, seen from the public terraces. The ever-present GCA position suggests that runway 06 is in use.

Societa Aereà Mediterranea was an Italian operator which was used for a number of years by tour operators for flights from Ringway. Their Douglas DC-6B I-DIME is shown here on 20 August 1964, with little visible activity at the Fairey Aviation site.

Mercury Airlines took delivery of their sole Dakota, G-AMSN, in April 1964. It was used on scheduled passenger services from Manchester and Liverpool, as well as charter services and newspaper flights from other airports, such as Birmingham. Seen at Ringway on 20 August 1964, flying ceased in October and the company was taken over by British Midland Airways Ltd.

Air France introduced the Sud Caravelle on the Paris-Manchester flight on 1 June 1961 and F-BHRO, named *Ile de France*, is about to depart from the International Pier of the new terminal *c*.1964.

Dan-Air operated eight Airspeed Ambassadors on Inclusive Tour work from a number of UK airports, including Ringway. They had purchased a number of Ambassadors, including surplus BEA aircraft. Taxiing in, during 1964, is G-AMAE.

The new terminal building came into use in December 1962 and the most striking features in the main concourse were the four Venetian-glass chandeliers. During a period of cleaning, the chandeliers were reduced in size and repositioned, the Traffic Hall having been remodelled over subsequent years. Seen in the background, by the windows overlooking the apron, is the Alcock and Brown memorial unveiled by the Lord Mayor of Manchester, dating this photograph after October 1964.

Swissair used Sud Aviation Caravelles on the Zurich service and brought HB-ICX to Ringway on 19 July 1965.

BEA started to use the Hawker Siddeley Trident One on flights to Paris from 1 July 1965 in place of Viscounts. Landing on 20 July 1965 is G-ARPH. A sister aircraft, G-ARPK, is presently used for ground safety training in the eastern dispersals at Ringway.

The west side of the International Pier was used mainly for the larger airliners and, on 25 July 1965, Sabena DC-6B OO-SDQ appears to have just arrived. A BOAC Boeing 707 is in the end bay.

Sabena substituted the Convair Metropolitans with Caravelles on the Brussels service in April 1964 and OO-SRB was used on 26 October 1965.

BOAC VC.10s G-ARVK and G-ARVB, on 14 December 1965, are likely to be diversions from Heathrow, both the VC.10 and Super VC.10 had been to Ringway on familiarization visits. The first scheduled non-stop transatlantic jet service from Manchester was inaugurated by BOAC with the Super VC.10 on 29 April 1969.

British Midland operated a small number of Canadair C-4 aircraft on charter work including Inclusive Tours. In its new livery, following renaming of the airline from Derby Airways, is G-ALHY during 1965.

Aer Lingus introduced their new fleet of BAC 1-11s to Ringway in June 1965, using them on flights through Manchester to the Continent, from Dublin to Amsterdam, Frankfurt, Dusseldorf and Copenhagen. Two Aer Lingus BAC 1-11s are on the International Pier, EI-ANF, named *St Malachy*, is nearest, with a BUA Dart Herald furthest away.

Britannia Airways Ltd had its origins in Euravia (London) Ltd, which was formed in 1961 using Lockheed Constellations through Ringway on Inclusive Tours. The airline purchased a number of Bristol Britannias from BOAC in 1964 and at this time changed its name to Britannia Airways. The aircraft were introduced into service from May 1965. Britannia Airways still operates from Manchester with a fleet of modern jet aircraft.

Dan-Air operated more than thirty de Havilland (Hawker Siddeley) Comets, having bought up surplus BEA and BOAC aircraft, as well as some from other airlines, to use on it's Inclusive Tour and other services. They were a frequent sight at Ringway. Seen here is G-APDK, which at one time served with BOAC. In the distance is the Fairey Aviation site now in the process of being put to other use, BEA having taken over one of the hangars.

British Eagle took delivery of BAC.1-11s in 1966 and G-ATPH in 1967. It was named *Salute*, and is seen at Ringway on 9 September 1967, leaving the International Pier. BEA Vanguards are in their regular spot.

BEA Viscount G-APIM, registration now shown in larger letters on the tail, unloading passengers immediately in front of the terminal building. Yewtree Lane used to run just past where this aircraft is parked on 2 October 1967.

BEA ordered the BAC 1-11 in 1967 and used the type on services from Heathrow and also their internal network in Germany, hence the revision in markings. Proving flights in and out of Ringway were started, many to Germany, but later in the year to Heathrow, replacing the Trident on this and a number of continental destinations. G-AVMN is in the original colour scheme on 18 May 1968. During 1971, BEA established the One-Eleven Division at Manchester, to maintain and control most of their services involving this type of aircraft.

Air Ferry Ltd had been set up at Manston Airport in Kent to operate Inclusive Tour flights for a local company and during 1968 leased two Vickers Viscounts from Channel Airways Ltd, one of which was G-AVNJ. The company closed down at the end of October 1968, its services being transferred to British United Airways.

BEA 1-11 G-AVMR, Caravelle Iberia EC-BIE and Laker 1-11 G-AVBW are lined up on the International Pier on 26 February 1969. Nose-in parking had not yet been introduced. In the far background, in front of Hangar No.522, are a few of the growing number of executive aircraft to be based at Ringway.

Air France Caravelle F-BHRD on 5 April 1969. The Caravelle was operated into Ringway by a number of airlines.

Britannia Airways standardized their fleet with the Boeing 737 in 1968 and, later in the year, used them on flights from Ringway. G-AVRM is seen here on 29 June 1969. The handling company Servisair began operations at Ringway in 1967, providing ground services, including passenger-handling, for a number of airlines.

As NEA began to build their air taxi business, larger aircraft were obtained, including Piper Aztecs and this Twin Comanche, G-AXDL, in 1969.

August 1970 saw the first visit of a BOAC Boeing 747 ,G-AWNC, on a demonstration flight, G-AWNA, the first aircraft in the BOAC order, came to Ringway on 2 September 1970. BOAC was not to operate the type on Manchester services until 1977, although they were seen regularly, due to Heathrow diversions and flights by other airlines.

BOAC Super VC.10 G-ASGM, departing runway 06 on 16 July 1971, shows the new administration block and Hangar No.6, used for cargo handling. BEA acted as agents for a number of airlines.

Oblique view taken from West, shows the 'Fairey' site, terminal building, piers, control tower block and the new extension office/administration block completed by 1971. Runway 24 improvements were made and the new fire station opened in 1970. Judging by the number of large aircraft present (BOAC 747s, VC.10s and 707s, El Al 747, Pan American 747, etc.) Ringway must have received diversions from Heathrow because of poor weather.

In October 1979 British Airways commissioned a de Havilland Dragon Rapide to be painted in their 'modern' colours. Normally based at Chirk, G-AKOE received these special markings for a ceremony at Manchester Airport on 28 October 1979, to mark the commencement of the British Airways shuttle service with BAC 1-11s to Heathrow.

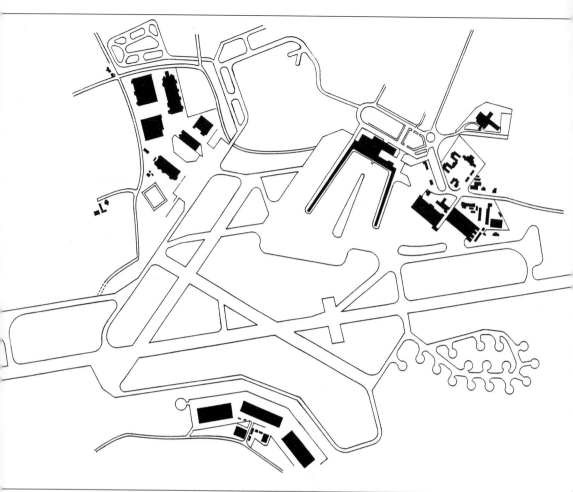

Manchester Airport c.1970.

Eight
Ringway Remembered

Few can now compare the modern airport with the early days but there are still links with the past, a number of original buildings remain and even recent development has revealed something of 'old' Ringway. Service organizations have also been remembered and a number of memorials exist in a specially-prepared memorial garden which is a credit to the Airport Authority.

Ringway had an air navigation beacon ordered before the beginning of the Second World War, eventually to be installed on the roof of what was to become Hangar No.7. The beacon provided a rotating white beam of light and a red flashing light to indicate the route to Ringway. It was taken out of use in later years, having been superceded by radio navigation aids, but remained on top of the hangar, disused, until the hangar was being demolished in early 1996. Realizing its historic importance, Tony Waites of Manchester Airport Airfield Systems (pictured), not only arranged its rescue but also its restoration and display in the airport terminal building.

Building 217 is the former RAF Station Officers Mess built during the war and converted in 1959 to office accommodation. Nearly all the buildings of RAF Ringway have now been demolished but '217' houses the Manchester Airport Archive which holds a considerable amount of information on the airport's history.

Hangars No.3 and No.4 on the Fairey site, now Western Maintenance Area, are the only survivors of their large site, used extensively by them both during, and after, the Second World War. The far hangar is used by the Airport Authority and the near hangar continues in use for aircraft maintenance. At one time it was the Danair Engineering base, later it was used by charter companies and airline operations. Both still have wartime air-raid warning posts built into the structure.

Now lost to the Second Runway development is this wartime 'pill box' used for airfield defence. There was a fear that enemy paratroops would make an airborne assault on Ringway and a number of pill boxes were constructed around the perimeter.

A more up to date Visual Control Room has replaced the original structure on the control tower, along with new radar, introduced to monitor ground movements. The extension to the control tower/administration block was fitted with black panels, which meant that the blue panels originally fitted to the control tower building were eventually replaced with black panels. The decorative concrete frieze is above the original entrance to the 1962 terminal building and all that can be seen externally of this building is now swallowed up by extensions.

Pier B (International) has not been rebuilt or developed in the same way as Pier A (Domestic) although much of it has been improved. The exterior frontage of gates 10, 12 and 14, apron flood-lighting masts and the area where spectators once had access are little altered.

No.613 (City of Manchester) Squadron, Royal Auxiliary Air Force, is commemorated by this new memorial which was unveiled by the Lord Mayor of Manchester, Councillor A.Burns, with a large number of the Squadron Association and guests, on 9 May 2000. The former pilots and squadron members continue to meet regularly.

Ringway was the wartime home of the RAF Central Landing Establishment which developed the use of glider and parachute techniques for airborne landings. It eventually became No.1 Parachute Training School of the RAF. Between 1942 and the end of the war it trained many personnel destined to join the Parachute Regiment, whose memorial is in the same garden area as No.613 Squadron's, with a number of other memorials.

A garden has been laid out near to Terminal One, to be used as a memorial garden and quiet area of the airport. Apart from services, it is used regularly by airport staff during their rest periods and lunch breaks.

Unusually quiet, the apron fronting the domestic side of Terminal One has just a Boeing 757 of British Airways, still in a colour scheme which is being replaced by a much brighter one. This is a regular parking spot for aircraft on the shuttle service to London Heathrow, July 2000.

On the ramp of Terminal Three, Gate 49, on 11 March 2000, is Boeing 737, G-XMAN, which shows both a new British Airways scheme, and a personalized registration.